Move On

Story by Melaina Faranda
Illustrations by Violet Tobacco

Move On

Text: Melaina Faranda
Publishers: Tania Mazzeo and Eliza Webb
Series consultant: Amanda Sutera
Hands on Heads Consulting
Editor: Jess Mackay
Project editor: Annabel Smith
Designer: Jess Kelly
Project designer: Danielle Maccarone
Illustrations: Violet Tobacco
Production controller: Renee Tome

NovaStar

ISBN 978 0 17 033513 3

Cengage Learning Australia
Level 5, 80 Dorcas Street
Southbank VIC 3006 Australia
Phone: 1300 790 853
Email: aust.nelsonprimary@cengage.com

For learning solutions, visit **cengage.com.au**

Printed in China by 1010 Printing International Ltd
1 2 3 4 5 6 7 29 28 27 26 25

Nelson acknowledges the Traditional Owners and Custodians of the lands of all First Nations Peoples. We pay respect to Elders past and present, and extend that respect to all First Nations Peoples today.

Contents

Chapter 1

Sold!

"But it was my birthday present from Dad. I still want to ride it. Please, Mum," Sasha begged. "Please!"

Mum barely glanced at her with those dazed, red-rimmed eyes that Sasha still hadn't got used to in the whole eight months since Dad died.

"Sold!" The man tried to make it sound like a joke, but he squirmed with discomfort under Sasha's glare as he unfolded two $100 notes from his wallet.

Mum hastily grabbed the notes and stuffed the money deep into her jeans pocket. She chased after him as he walked down the driveway wheeling Sasha's sky-blue bike. "Are you interested in buying one for a younger child as well?"

The man shook his head and picked up his pace, before swiftly loading the bike onto the tray of his shiny black ute, where a girl Sasha's age beamed excitedly from the passenger seat.

There had been pity in the man's eyes. It made Sasha burn with shame. This wasn't the first time she'd noticed people who'd come to buy their things looking at Mum, and then at her and the twins, Charlie and Lily, with that same expression. She stared after the ute as it turned the corner and vanished with her bike. Would the girl ride it along the bike path with her father like Sasha had with Dad on their Sunday mornings?

Dad had given her the bike on her birthday, only a month before he died, saying she was too old for the one she'd been riding for the past few years. Together, they had sped away from the chaos of the twins wreaking havoc and strewing toys around, and towards the cafe in the park – the one place where Mum's healthy-eating rules didn't apply.

Dad used to secretly let Sasha have a hot chocolate with marshmallows. It had started with them sharing. Dad said he'd only let her have one of her own if she could pronounce the word "froth" correctly.

"Froff. Froff. Froth." From the day she could say "froth" properly, he'd always ordered her a whole mug.

They usually talked about Sasha's school and who was popular and who wasn't, how Sasha was going with her hockey team, and what her dreams for the future were. Sasha wished that she had asked Dad questions about himself. If she had, she might now have more memories of him to hold onto.

"Come inside now, Sasha," Mum called from the doorway. "It's going to get dark soon."

Sasha waited until Mum had gone in, her blood boiling with rage. Since Charlie and Lily's arrival four years ago, life had been chaotic. Dad was always kept busy working or fixing things or trying to give each of them snatches of his time. Now, Mum had just sold the one precious thing Sasha had shared with Dad. She stood, arms folded across her chest, as the sun sank behind the buildings across the street. The summer air mercifully grew cooler, and Sasha crept back into the house.

Inside, if it were possible, the place was even bleaker than in those first weeks after Dad had the heart attack that killed him.

Sasha felt the absence of his booming tickle-monster voice as he chased the twins and her (though she protested she was twelve now and too old) around the house until they all dissolved into a giggling heap on the big seven-seater sofa. The comfiest couch in the world, Dad declared.

That sofa had been sold to a lady who had sniffed at it suspiciously and checked that the legs hadn't been chewed by a puppy. But there was no puppy. Mum and Dad had promised they would get one when the twins were a bit older, but Sasha knew there would never be one now.

Every day, for months, she'd returned home from school to discover that familiar things were gone. It was strange, this feeling of disorientation, like some kind of horrible guessing game. Something would feel out of place or not quite right. Sasha scanned each room until she discovered what was missing. The garage was already empty. To help pay for the funeral, Dad's pride and joy – his motorbike – had been sold within days of his heart attack. The tropical fish aquariums followed soon after. Having her father's things go was tough but at least they had been stored largely out of sight in the garage. It wasn't the same as having things vanish from inside the house.

As much as she could, Sasha found reasons to visit other people after school. It was easy to do. She was good at telling amazing stories and inventing new games. Friends enjoyed having her around. Increasingly, Sasha stayed at their houses for as long as she could in the afternoons. She wanted to try and avoid the sickening feeling of coming home, only to discover more of their lives with Dad were missing. It was as if someone had taken a giant eraser and started to rub out how things had once been.

Charlie and Lily lay sprawled together on a fluffy blanket in the living room, watching cartoons on the television (before it, too, would be sold). In the kitchen, Mum sat hunched over a cup of tea, staring into mid-air at something only she could see. The past? A different future to the one they faced now? Sasha knew that the tea was probably already cold, and that Mum would have used the same teabag for the third time.

There were no fresh Earl Grey tea leaves now – they couldn't afford them. And the vintage green teapot in the shape of an old woman who lived in a shoe had been sold. As had Mum's collection of china teacups and saucers.

"Mum?" Sasha said.

Mum was startled, slopping the tea onto the spotless bench. Sasha glimpsed the glitter of unshed tears. "Oh, Sasha Bear, I'm so, so sorry about your bike. We needed the money."

At the familiar sound of Dad's nickname for her, Sasha's fury dissolved. "Do you want me to get Charlie and Lily into the bath?"

Mum's voice became brisk and efficient as she reached for a cloth and cleaned up the spill. "It's all right, love. I'll do it. You've got school tomorrow. Don't you have that history project you're working on?"

"It's the weekend," Sasha said. "Remember? It's the last week of school before the holidays."

"Is it?"

Without Dad's income, and since she'd lost her job, Mum had been unable to afford day care for Charlie and Lily. It seemed as if she often didn't even know what day of the week it was.

Sasha had overheard Mum on the phone to Krista, a childhood friend who lived up the coast and who Mum hadn't seen for years. When Krista had learned about Dad's death, she'd made contact and quickly became Mum's main support. They talked on the phone together nearly every other night.

Sasha guessed that Krista must have said something about how awful it was for Mum's company to fire her after she had been widowed. But Mum had said the company was already downsizing. Hers was just one of a whole round of job losses.

After the funeral, it turned out that they were truly alone. Mum had always said she was too busy for anything other than what she had always wanted: a great job and a husband and kids she could have only ever dreamed of.

For the first few weeks after Dad's heart attack, some of the school parents dropped around baked goods and dishes, but then that stopped. The busy, efficient, organised Mum who Sasha remembered would have always known what day of the week it was. But during the months since Dad died, that version of Mum also seemed to be vanishing, along with their things.

Now Sasha sighed. She tried to hide her frustration. "In a week, I'm meant to be going away with Clare's family to the Big Three theme parks. They want to leave on the Saturday after school finishes."

Mum shook her head, as if rousing herself from sleep. For the first time in a while, she directly met Sasha's eyes. "Actually, I need to talk with you about that. You won't be going."

Chapter 2

Car-camping

Sasha stared open-mouthed with disbelief. Not only would she not be going with Clare on holidays, but Mum had just said they would be moving house and changing schools!

"So, since we're moving, we wouldn't be able to take the bike with us anyway," Mum finished.

Sasha didn't know how to respond. "Moving? But where?"

"Up to Krista's. She lives near the beach. It's always so much warmer up there and I just won't be able to afford the heating bills here during winter. Krista's offered to put us up while I look for somewhere else, something smaller, to rent. She says there are plenty of empty places sitting around after the school holidays are over."

"But I'm meant to be going away with Clare!"

Mum sighed. "The thing is, Sasha, I just can't

afford to keep living here. I'm already a month behind on rent. If we leave now, before we're evicted, I stand a chance of the real estate agent giving me a good reference."

"You're just going to pull me out of school?" Sasha's voice rose. "Away from my friends? What about hockey? What about how ... how we lived here with Dad!"

"I'm sorry, Sasha Bear–"

"Don't call me that! That's Dad's name for me!"

"Sweetheart, I don't see that I have any other choice. I've tried to keep you sheltered from all this and I've been selling what I can, but–"

"You don't think I notice how things go missing all the time?" Sasha asked incredulously. "You just sold my birthday bike that Dad gave to me. Why can't Grandma and Grandpa help?"

This was a low blow. Mum had rarely spoken about these mythical-seeming people, let alone ever called them Grandma and Grandpa. Sasha wished she had the kind of grandparents some of her friends had. Ones who lived close by and regularly picked their grandkids up from ballet and soccer and had big Christmas feasts and bought too many presents and clearly thought their grandkids were the best thing ever.

Dad's parents lived in England. They seemed nice enough over the video calls Dad had sometimes made to them, and they always sent Sasha cards with toadstools and squirrels and bluebells on them for her birthday. But they were pensioners and hadn't even been able to afford the airfares to travel to their only son's funeral.

It had been Dad who'd once confided in Sasha, when she'd asked for the hundredth time about her other grandparents, that Mum's relationship with them was complicated. Mum had decided it was for the best to not have them in her own children's lives and when Dad died, they didn't even send a card.

Sasha aimed one last kick. "If you're pulling me out of school, why did you even bother telling me to do my history project?"

Mum's shoulders slumped. Any fight drained out of her. She put her head in her hands and spoke in a small voice. "I just can't see any other way. We're about to be evicted. We have to move on."

"When are we leaving?" Sasha asked in a small, tight voice, not trusting that she wouldn't start screaming at her mother and never stop.

"Next Saturday, the day after school breaks."

In the passenger seat beside Mum, Sasha clutched Ellie: the worn-out stuffed elephant she'd had since babyhood. Ellie was wearing the school shirt that had been freshly signed by her friends with permanent markers. It was the last day of the school year, and there had been tears. The teacher had even brought in a cake.

Behind her, in amongst pillows and blankets, Charlie and Lily clutched their own toys and a couple of picture books. Charlie had a train and Lily held her lion. Mum had allowed them to bring one toy each, along with a small stack of picture books. Otherwise, with all the bags and boxes loaded onto the mattress in the back of the station wagon, there was no room.

Sasha silently said goodbye to their street and life as she had always known it. They passed the mulberry tree where Charlie and Lily had turned purple while cramming berries into their mouths; the little glass-fronted yellow cupboard of a community book exchange; Howard, the friendly, fat golden retriever with his four paws dangling in the air, catching the sun in a neighbour's driveway; the house with the turret that Mum had laughingly told Dad was her dream house and how she was going to need to get a promotion to pay for it; and the park where Dad had endlessly pushed two swings in response to the twins clamouring for more!

"Alright?" Mum asked with a false cheerfulness belied by her own face, which was a pale mask of conflicting worries.

Sasha nodded.

"Tonight, we car-camp!" Mum announced brightly. "We're having an adventure."

In the back, Charlie and Lily looked up from their picture books with uncertainty.

Mum flashed Sasha a pleading look.

"Yay!" Sasha called out, to which the twins immediately chimed in: "Yay!"

There was only so much I Spy with My Little Eye that could be played with two four year olds who couldn't actually spell. After Charlie had stumped everyone with "k" for "clock", Mum mercifully gave it a rest.

Sasha watched as the countryside sped by – the edge of the city giving way to flat, grey-green fields and patches of forest.

Just before dark, Mum pulled onto a dirt road. They jolted along a bumpy track riddled with puddles and potholes, until they finally arrived at a forest glade. Across the small circular clearing were silhouettes of people huddled around a campfire. Orange flames licked and sparked up into the deep blue evening, towards the first sprinkling of stars.

Sasha inhaled fresh tree-and-smoke scented air, a welcome change after the stuffy car heater. “Where did you find out about this place?”

Mum smiled tiredly. “Online. It’s a free camping spot. I didn’t want to stop at a caravan park. We need to conserve our funds.” She added: “Time to feed the monsters.”

But Charlie and Lily were both fast asleep. Sasha helped Mum recline the front seats, unclip the twins and gently transfer them. They barely stirred as Mum put blankets over them.

The orange glow of the distant campfire emphasised the deep lines of weariness in Mum’s face as she fetched a plastic tub with the cooking pots. She looked ready to fall over from tiredness.

Sasha yawned to hide her grumbling stomach. “Actually, Mum, I’m not that hungry.”

“Really?” Mum was unable to disguise her relief. “Are you sure? I can make us eggs?”

“No, I’d just like to sleep.”

Mum nodded and together they pulled the boxes off the mattress and clambered onto it. As Mum fumbled to pull the boot door down from the inside, she promised: "We'll have a big breakfast in the morning."

Only with the regular rhythm of Mum's breathing in her sleep did Sasha allow herself to fully feel. All day, she'd been trying her hardest to plaster on a happy face, to act like it really was an adventure on the school holidays. But now, the reality of what had just happened, what was still to happen, came crashing down.

They had left home. She had said goodbye to her friends and the school where she had topped English and her teacher had praised her for having such a vivid imagination, even entering a story Sasha had written into a schoolwide competition that had won second prize.

Everything had been sold. What couldn't be sold was given to charity shops: her bed, the ornaments she'd gathered and been gifted over the years and her desk with the little blue porcelain-and-brass knobs. Her books had been left in a box beneath the community book exchange.

The house she had lived in since she was a baby would be lived in by another family. Everything was gone.

Even worse was the fact that home was where she had the most memories of Dad. How long before they would be gone, too?

Chapter 3

Beach Holiday

They had driven for two full days and car-camped at night before finally arriving at Krista's house. A wide arc of deep green river flowed into the ocean beyond. Bordering the river was a park with slides and swing sets. Coastal pines towered over the park, where brightly coloured birds shrieked noisily from the branches.

Mum pulled the car over to the side of the road to phone Krista. "Hi!" she said brightly. "We've just pulled in now."

Mum suddenly became silent. Her forehead creased as she listened to Krista on the other end. "Yes, I understand. But even for just a couple of nights?"

There was more silence, then Mum said, "Please, Krista, I'm begging. We've come all this way! I have no savings. Nothing. Until I get a job there's only enough to feed the kids."

Mum was deathly pale as she fumbled to put the phone back into the console.

"What is it?" Sasha demanded.

"Krista says it's not going to be possible to stay with her after all."

"You said she'd offered for us to stay until we could find somewhere to rent," Sasha accused.

"Things have changed."

"But why?"

Mum was tight-lipped. "I don't want to go into this with you, Sasha. Not now."

On cue, as if they had sensed the tension, Charlie and Lily began to fight. They were bored, cranky and howling as they whacked each other with their toys.

Sasha shoved the car door open and unclipped the twins from their booster seats. She was furious. How could Mum have been so stupid to rely on a friend she hadn't seen for years? "I'll take them to the park while *you* figure this out."

But Mum had no answers. While Sasha put a hand around Charlie and Lily's shoulders to march them to the park, Mum said she would look around the town for any job notices posted in shop windows.

Sasha had given up on pushing swings and was instead keeping an eye on the twins poking sticks at ants when Mum finally returned to the park nearly an hour later.

She seemed cheerful. “I spotted quite a few ads looking for cleaners. There must be a lot of money in this town if everyone wants cleaners.
I should be able to get work easily here.”

“What about places to live?” Sasha asked.

Mum’s face fell again. “I checked out the real estate windows for places to rent but it’s the school holidays. Most of the properties are short-term rentals right now and too expensive.”

“So where are we going to stay?” Sasha insisted.

“Sasha Bear, I’m really sorry but it might be a couple more nights in the car until I can secure work and put out the word to locals that we’re looking for somewhere.”

Sasha did not want to spend another night in the car. “Maybe we could move somewhere else?”

Mum shook her head. “It’s a nice town and in winter it will be warm. I’ve heard the schools here are good. Frankly, I’m tired. We’ve got to make a go of it somewhere. It may as well be here. I honestly don't know if I have the stamina to keep looking."

It didn't turn out to be just one more night in the car. More like a succession of nights while Mum waited to hear back about the cleaning jobs. In the mornings, they all went to the beach before it was taken over by the striped umbrellas and sun shelters of happy families on school holidays.

Sometimes they'd tumble out of the car at dawn and walk through the sleepy streets to the break wall – a gravel path stretching across huge jumbled boulders that separated the beach from the river mouth.

Each of those times, an older lady cycled past them on a bike covered with rainbow-coloured crocheted patches and handlebars wrapped in fake flowers and streaming ribbons. Her long silver hair streamed out from beneath a bike helmet covered in knitted flowers and huge fabric daisies. She waved at the twins when they stopped to stare, enchanted.

Mum had packed their swimming costumes

and bought a couple of cheap floaty toys for the twins. Charlie had a purple-and-green dinosaur and Lily a rainbow-coloured unicorn. Sitting in the golden sunshine and listening to seagulls and the gentle swish of the sea lapping the shore, Sasha was almost able to pretend it really was a holiday.

Afterwards, they all showered in the outdoor showers and, when there was no one around, Mum quickly washed the twins' hair. There was a caravan park on the shore, but Mum felt too embarrassed to find out from any of the holidaymakers the keypad code for the amenities block. She had asked around to see if there were any community services, but the nearest centre was over two hours away.

Even with Mum's dedication to healthy eating, it was impossible to keep food cold in the car, so they mostly ate cereal and long-life milk for breakfast and sandwiches for lunch.

During the late afternoon, Sasha did her best to chase the twins up and down the slides and push each of them on the swings near the river park while Mum cooked on the barbecues. Later, when it was dark, Mum turned the car up roads without streetlights. They parked in a different street each night. That way, Mum said, people were less likely to notice them and complain.

She had fiercely instructed Sasha that she was never to mention they were living in the car. "It will just be for as long as it takes me to get work and then a place to rent. I don't know what would happen if people thought I couldn't provide a proper house for you. The authorities might take you and the twins away."

Chapter 4

Good News

The good news came on day five when a lady rang to offer Mum an interview for a job cleaning luxury holiday homes. Mum was nervous as she dropped Sasha and the twins off at the library. “If anyone asks you where your parents are, say you’re visiting your aunty from interstate.”

Sasha nestled in with Charlie and Lily, reading them what must’ve been the twentieth picture book they’d chosen, and trying to do the voices like Dad had. A little while later, she heard Mum’s voice at the reception desk. She listened anxiously and then relaxed, realising her mother’s tone was light and cheerful.

Outside, on the pavement, Mum jumped up and down. “I got the job! I got it.” Charlie and Lily caught the excitement and raced in small, tight circles around Mum's legs. "It's not great pay, but the woman agreed that Charlie and Lily can come with me while I clean until I can get them into childcare. It means now I can enrol you in school, too," Mum said. "Come on, let's all get a celebratory gelato!"

As she licked her double-choc, toffee-crunch gelato, Sasha asked the question that had been burning inside her this whole time. "When will we be able to live in a real house?"

Mum's face fell. "Oh, Sasha Bear, I'll need to work for a few weeks to save up the rental bond and deposit."

"So we have to live in the car until then?"

A shadow crossed Mum's face.

On cue, Charlie dropped his ice cream and started to howl. Mum instantly knelt, scraped up the scoop and plonked it back onto his cone. "Three second rule," she said guiltily.

But Sasha was equally beside herself. "How am I going to manage to do my homework?" she asked. "And where do I say I'm living? You said we can't tell anyone."

"It won't be for long, Sasha. I promise."

"You promised we wouldn't be in the car and look what happened to that promise."

Sasha wished she could take the words back. But it was too late - Mum's eyes closed and she fell silent. As they walked to the river park, Mum quietly dropped her own ice cream into the bin.

Later, when Mum was cooking sausages over at the barbecue, Lily screamed that there was a spider. As Sasha dealt with the spider, Charlie took the opportunity to run to the river's edge where he tumbled down onto rocks crusted in oyster shells exposed by the low tide.

Sasha managed to haul up the bawling, inconsolable four year old covered in blood, thankful that he hadn't fallen into the river.

Mum raced over, panicking. And just then, the older lady with the colourful bicycle covered in knitted flowers came riding past. The moment she saw Charlie, she braked, dropped her bike to the grass and rushed towards them. "What happened?" she said.

"I don't know. He fell over at the river," Sasha said, her throat tight with terror. "He's bleeding everywhere."

The woman narrowed her eyes and assessed him carefully. "Oyster cuts," she pronounced. "They'll only be shallow, but they're razor sharp. We'll need to disinfect them. Don't want them getting infected by any nasties. Where are you staying?" she asked Mum.

Mum shook her head. "We're um … camping."

"Have you got a first aid kit?"

Mum looked stricken.

"Never mind. I've got some antiseptic solution back where I am. I used to be a nurse." She added: "By the way, my name's Maggie. Some people around here call me Magic Maggie."

"Thanks, Maggie," Mum said, her voice thick with gratitude.

"I live a little too far for you all to walk. Especially with this young man in the state that he's in. Would you be happy to follow me in your car?" Maggie glanced straight over at their car, one of twenty or more parked in the car park.

Sasha realised in the same moment that Maggie had probably noticed a lot more than she was saying. She already knew that they were sleeping in the car.

"Just to warn you, the road can be a bit rough."

Chapter 5

Secret Camp

At the end of a long dirt road, hidden within scrubland and tucked behind coastal dunes, was a hidden camp. There were a couple of vans, two cars with tarp awnings hung off the side, a few tents and a big silver bus with window boxes filled with parsley, chives and basil. The destination panel at the front of the bus featured, in big block letters, the word **MAGIC**.

Maggie had ridden her bike ahead of them, neatly swerving past the ruts and potholes. She climbed up into the silver bus and emerged again waving a first aid kit.

Sasha took in their surroundings as Maggie tenderly wiped away streaks of blood and dabbed antiseptic onto the thin cuts on Charlie's calves and shins.

"Thank you so much," Mum said.

Maggie smiled. "My pleasure. Reckon I've done this so many times I could do it in my sleep."

"What is this place?" Sasha asked.

"Ah yes, glad you asked that," Maggie replied. "But first I have to know if you can keep a secret?"

Sasha straightened her shoulders and stuck out her chin. Naturally she could keep a secret – isn't that what Mum had been asking her to do this whole time?

"This is a magical place where people come to live freely. It's only moments from those million-dollar houses up on the hills, but it's as close to the river and the beach as you could possibly be. The bird song is louder and sweeter here and, at night, you can go to sleep listening to the sea singing lullabies."

Sasha frowned, uncertain if Maggie was using one of those "let's pretend" adult voices, but the older lady's grey eyes were filled with genuine delight.

"Who lives here?" Mum asked.

"Travellers, free spirits and, if you'd like, people like you." Maggie nodded. "But only people who've been invited. This is private land, so we can't get kicked out. A friend I met on a campaign inherited it. The plan had been to develop, bulldoze and plaster it with a hundred houses, but these are sensitive wetlands, and my friend has seen the light."

Mum nodded slowly, trying to take it all in as Maggie added, "We still try and lie low though. My friend doesn't want to be hassled by the council."

Sasha piped up. "But how do you choose who can stay here?"

Maggie smiled. "I've been keeping an eye on you all. Been a bit worried about a mum with three kids out there all on your own."

She turned back to Mum. "I can see you've been doing your best, sweetheart. It can be tough out there. I've already talked to the others, and you're welcome to join us here if you like."

"Here?" Mum repeated. "You mean stay here?"

"As long as you like."

"But I'm looking for a house to rent," Mum said. "I just got a job. Sasha will be going to school. I don't plan on living in a car with my kids forever."

Maggie smiled. "Like I said – however long you like. Cup of tea?" She climbed back up into the bus and gestured for them to follow.

Inside the silver bus was a wonderland. Maggie's bike was decorated with crocheted patches and flowers, but the interior of the bus was an even wilder kaleidoscope of colours. Strands of beads, peacock feathers and giant fabric flowers hung from the walls above a big bed. There was a potbelly stove up one end, plants with tendrils and shelves crammed with a teacup collection to rival Mum's before it had been sold.

Maggie happily slurped tea that she'd poured straight from a pot sporting a knitted mushroom tea cosy. "You'd be surprised how much can be healed with a nice cup of tea. And I say that as a nurse. Well, ex-nurse now that I've retired."

Charlie and Lily sat on the shiny patchwork quilt on Maggie's bed, cheerfully tangling up balls of yarn, while Mum sipped dazedly, as if in a dream. It was Sasha who listened intently, while dunking a ginger-nut biscuit into the peppermint tea Maggie had made especially for her.

Maggie said she had never married or had children and, apart from her patients at work, there had only been herself to take care of. She had once owned a nice house in the suburbs

where everything was mostly shades of white and kept hospital-grade clean. She'd worked for over forty years in the same hospital painted similar shades of white. And the whole time she had wondered – is this all there is?

Maggie said she'd discovered she was bored when she retired, until one day she was amazed by a protest march that spilled through the street where she was out shopping. In the middle of the rally, a group of older women in brightly coloured knitted and crocheted ensembles carried a banner: Knitting Nannas for the Planet. These were women who knitted at and for protests. Maggie followed them to where the march ended in a rally and signed up on the spot.

Within weeks, anywhere the Earth and its creatures were in threat of being harmed – Maggie was there. Her knitting and crocheted designs became increasingly bright and multicoloured, and she became so committed that she bought the silver bus to travel from demonstration to demonstration. There were defender camps to save thousand-year-old rainforests from being logged. She had chained herself to an old piano filled with cement, rowed out in a crochet-covered kayak to surround a navy ship, sat in circles around campfires, and chopped endless amounts of carrots and pumpkins and potatoes to make curries to feed hungry activists.

Over time, Maggie said, she realised that she didn't miss her home in the suburbs one single bit. "The thing is, for most of human history, no one lived in houses. It's not natural to be glued to a screen when we could be looking up at the stars." She sold her house and its mostly white furniture and gave the proceeds to a wildlife conservation fund. Since then, Maggie had been living in the magic bus and happier than ever.

"I'm just one old woman who wants to make a difference before I die. My motto is: adventure before dementia."

Mum burst into laughter. "That's a wonderful credo!"

Noting Sasha's expression, Mum explained: "Dementia is when people start to lose their memories."

But Sasha already knew what dementia was. What had surprised her was the sound of Mum's genuine laughter.

It wasn't the sound she made to pretend to the twins that she was having a good time, but a lovely, rich pealing that Sasha hadn't heard since Dad had died.

"You'll find some real characters here," Maggie said to them both. "And everyone has a story. You have a story, too. One day I hope you might share it with me."

Chapter 6

How the Rich Live

Although they were introduced to people while setting up their camp, it was only over the weekly shared meal that Sasha, Mum and the twins met everyone properly.

Through the gentle murmuring around the campfire, Sasha discovered that a few of the people were professional environmental activists, taking a break between campaigns. There was a tanned couple from Ecuador with gentle white smiles, an old guy with a tie knotted through his shorts named Ken who'd once been a stockman out west, and a young mother with a tiny baby in a fabric pouch tied across her chest.

People smiled when Charlie and Lily raced circles around the fire. They shared a little bit about their lives without grilling Mum or Sasha about theirs. Later that night, Mum and Sasha sat up and gazed at a thrilling spill of stars.

"Beats the glow-in-the-dark plastic ones I had stuck on my ceiling," Sasha said.

Mum laughed. "Have you noticed how happy the little monsters are being outside so much?"

"It's good," Sasha agreed. "They don't wake up during the night any more." Whether that was because they were all tuckered out or because they felt safe and snug cocooned in the car with Mum and Sasha was unknown. Perhaps it was both.

Mum had been allocated a space that led into the bushes. A few days after arriving, she was able to string up sarongs to make a bush shower and, on Maggie's recommendation, she bought a cheap tent to store their things and a portable toilet, too.

To give Mum a quick break, Sasha sometimes took the twins with her to visit Maggie in her silver bus. Sasha would sit and drink peppermint tea while Maggie chattered about her many adventures.

It took some time for Sasha to talk about her own life and stories she'd made up.

“You have a wonderful imagination,” Maggie said. She nodded towards the twins who were demolishing another ball of yarn. “If you ever need the space to write your stories, you’re welcome to come over here when I’m out.”

If Maggie wasn’t there, Mum wasn’t prepared to leave Sasha alone in the camp with the twins. With still a few weeks to go before school started, they all piled into the car and Sasha was lumped with twin-sitting while Mum whisked around cleaning hilltop mansions worth millions of dollars.

Some of the houses were so big they would take Mum two whole days to clean. There were infinity pools, jacuzzi spas, helicopter pads, saunas, kabanas, steam rooms, games rooms, private cinemas and baths so deep you could practically swim in them. One house even had giant boulders and a waterfall in the living room.

Some of the houses were rented out and others belonged to company directors, movie stars and people from overseas who might visit only once or twice a year, but the house still had to be kept clean the whole time, in case the owners felt like flying in for a day.

For those houses, huge floral displays were delivered weekly by the florists, only for the flowers to wither and die unseen and be thrown out and replaced with new arrangements. The fridges had to be kept stocked with fresh gourmet food. Mum had to check the expiry dates.

When something had gone out of date, Mum was meant to throw it in the bin, but if it wasn't off she snuck it back to the camp instead. It was crazy; those houses, some with restaurant-grade kitchens, were a world away from the one they lived in back at the camp, where Mum fried barely out-of-date food on a portable gas camping stove and served it up on mismatched plates.

Maggie would occasionally accept the smuggled food, while shaking her head with disgust. "It's such a waste how the rich live. It's insane. No wonder the planet can't cope."

But for all her disapproval of people consuming unnecessarily, Maggie did support Sasha's plea for new clothes to start school with. "That kind of thing is important to kids. Sasha needs to be able to go to school and hold her head high."

Maggie had even offered to pay, but Mum refused. "You've done enough for us already."

Buying new clothes and school equipment meant Mum had to use the food bank that week. They had lined up for free lunches in the community hall, but Maggie pointed out that so did dozens of others and that it was no fault of Mum's that Dad had died. He'd had an unexpected heart attack. Maggie said that everyone knew times were tough and what kind of world was it where some people flew helicopters to have lunch, while others had to live in their cars?

Chapter 7

New School

Sasha was up even earlier than the twins for the first day of school. The evening before, she had washed her hair beneath the bush shower behind the screen of sarongs.

Sasha asked Mum to braid her hair and checked, once again, in the car's side mirror that she looked normal; that she was just like any other girl who lived in a real house, with clean clothes and neatly cut sandwiches in her lunchbox.

All of the kids in Sasha's class were returning students. She was the only new girl in their whole year.

The teacher, Mr Brock, assigned a girl called Ebony to help Sasha get to know her way around the school. They weren't allowed to talk in class.

It was only during the break that Ebony, joined by her friend, Maya, was able to ask, "Where have you moved to? Our house is on Shell Street." Ebony pulled out a thick piece of carrot cake with cream-cheese icing from her lunchbox.

Maya opened her lunchbox to reveal neat circles of sushi. "Our place is on Wave Street," she said. "Which street are you on?"

Sasha had already picked up on the way that nearly every street in the town was named after something to do with the beach. Now, she panicked. No way she could say she wasn't living on a street, but along a rough dirt track to a secret place in the bush. Oh yeah, that's right, and it wasn't actually a house she lived in, but a car ...

Before she knew it, Sasha rattled off the address of one of the mansions Mum cleaned at night. She could hardly forget it because the street name and number had been made a feature with inset lights that glowed in curving stone walls.

The girls looked impressed.

"That's where the really posh houses are," Maya said.

Embarrassed at having lied, Sasha tried

to downplay it. "We haven't been there very long. What kind of things do you like to do after school?"

But Ebony wouldn't let it go. "What's your house like?" she pressed. "Has it got an infinity pool where it looks like the water is going straight over the edge into the ocean?"

Sasha nodded. Strictly speaking that wasn't exactly a lie. Even if it wasn't her place, the house did have an infinity pool just like that.

Ebony's eyes were shining.

Sasha took a deep breath. "It's got a heated spa and a slide that goes into it, too. There's a big floating bar sort of thing in the centre and a sauna and steam room."

"Wow," Ebony breathed. "Your family must be really rich."

Slowly, Sasha nodded. It felt wrong to be lying but so good to finally be someone else. Instead of being someone these girls would pity – a kid who ate from food banks and slept in a car on a mattress next to her mum, while her brother and sister slept in the front seats – she could be a rich kid with an infinity pool. And one with two parents.

"My dad owns a company," she said. "We've got

houses all around the world. Dad flies a helicopter, so sometimes we just fly between houses."

"No offence," Maya said, "but why aren't you wearing designer clothes?"

Sasha blushed, suddenly ashamed of the no-name clothes Mum had bought brand new from the department store, which she had felt so good about only that morning. Was it that obvious?

She thought quickly. "My parents don't like us looking any different. They said it can make people feel bad if they can't afford the same stuff, so they just get us to wear ordinary clothes."

She added, "It's the same with schools. They want us to be able to fit in with everybody."

The girls seemed momentarily satisfied with this explanation but, keen to distract them and anxious to change the subject, Sasha asked, "Do people play hockey here?"

Ebony beamed. "I do! You should join our team."

When Sasha arrived back at the camp after school that afternoon, Mum rushed to give her a hug. "How was it? Did everything go okay? Do you like your teacher? Did you make any friends?"

Sasha peeled herself away from Mum's embrace. "It was okay."

It was only later, when sharing a peppermint tea with Maggie, while Mum sponge-washed the twins before bed, that Sasha wanted to talk about what Mr Brock was like (mostly strict) and meeting Ebony and Maya.

Maggie listened attentively. "Sounds like you've got off to a great start. I know you'll be needing to do homework, so you're always welcome to come over here when I'm out riding in the afternoons." She gestured towards what might have been a desk under a tangle of ribbons and raffia, silk flowers and teacups. "The Magic Bus is never locked."

Chapter 8

Sleepover

Sasha could barely contain her excitement. When Mr Brock asked what had got into her and why she kept shifting in her chair, she couldn't answer him properly.

She and Maya were having a sleepover that night at Ebony's, for Ebony's birthday. It would be the first real family house Sasha had been in since they had left their own.

Over the past few weeks, Sasha had become closer with the two girls. She had tried to avoid talking any further about her "mansion", but each time one of them asked she couldn't help but give more details.

She talked about the massive flower arrangements that were delivered each week and how Dad had friends in the movies who got early access to the latest films. She said they watched them together as a family while eating burnt-caramel popcorn from their own machine in their private underground cinema.

Although she felt guilty about lying, every time she spoke about it and saw her friends' awe, Sasha felt as if she was able to believe that, just for the briefest moment, her life really was this fairy tale. Especially when she got to mention Dad as if he were still alive.

She had told Ebony and Maya that Dad's chauffeur took her to school early because he had to drop Dad off at the airport where Dad flew to work in his private jet.

In reality, it meant that she was anxious to get to school each morning before anyone else. Then, in the afternoon, Sasha waited until all the buses had already gone and most of the kids had been picked up by their parents, before taking the shortcut through the bushes back to the camp.

After that first day of school, Sasha had insisted that Mum didn't try to drop her off or pick her up, knowing that Ebony and Maya would take one look at Mum's car with the mattress in the back and know that Sasha had been lying.

When Mum had argued with her, Sasha

snapped, “I don’t want you coming because it’s too embarrassing.” She had felt bad, but she was desperate to keep Mum away.

On their walk from school to Ebony’s house, Ebony apologised for her house, saying it was nothing like Sasha’s mansion.

They arrived at the entrance to a two-storey house where a cute cavoodle called Baci bounded to greet them with leaps and licks. There was a swimming pool out the back and scented candles everywhere.

Ebony’s mum was just finishing a yoga session in front of the TV. She rolled up her mat and greeted Sasha with a warm smile. “You must be Sasha. It’s lovely to meet you. Ebony has told me so much about you. Now, how would you girls like to make some chocolate-chip cookies?”

Ebony looked embarrassed. “Sasha has a personal chef from France, Mum. I don’t think she’ll care about cooking.”

Ebony’s mother tilted her head and examined Sasha quizzically. “A French chef?”

Sasha swiftly mumbled, “Just sometimes. But my mum likes to cook, too.” She didn’t add: mostly expired gourmet food over a camp stove.

“Where did you say you lived?”

Sasha quickly rattled off the address.

"C'mon, Eb," Maya said. "I'm hungry. Let's make the cookies!"

There was an actual mixer, cake beaters and a real oven. The girls got dough everywhere and when Sasha grabbed a cloth to clean crumbs and flour from the bench, Ebony said to leave it for her mum. Sasha frowned. She was so used to helping her own mother.

"We should really do it ourselves. It's not fair to make someone else do it."

"But don't you have maids and cleaners and stuff at your place to do all that?" Maya asked.

Sasha couldn't answer with the truth: her mother really *was* the cleaner.

They traipsed upstairs to Ebony's room to wait while the cookies baked. Sasha looked around enviously. Ebony had a double bed teeming with throw cushions and a screen that she could watch from bed. There were pretty lamps, framed pictures and hockey trophies on the shelf. Ebony had a walk-in wardrobe and another door into her own private ensuite.

Back in the camp, Sasha had a plastic tub in a tent that housed all their clothes and food.

If she needed to go to the toilet, it was either

go in the bushes or in a portable toilet that Mum then emptied once a week at the disposal place in the caravan park.

“Want to watch a movie?” Ebony asked. “I mean, I know it’s not like being in your own cinema.”

Sasha nodded, enchanted. She hadn’t watched anything on a screen bigger than Mum’s phone since before they had left home.

At some stage, Sasha managed to stop feeling guilty about Mum and the twins, and instead fully relaxed by being in a real house.

She used nearly every single shampoo and soap product in the bathroom and stood under the hot shower so long that Ebony banged on the door for her to hurry up because they were going to start another movie.

It felt amazing to just switch lights on and not worry that the car battery would go flat, and to use the toilet without having to take a torch and worry about snakes or spiders in the bushes. And, most of all, it felt wonderful to have a bed all to herself. Maya slept beside Ebony in the double bed while Sasha got to sleep in the pull-out trundle bed, made up with freshly washed and ironed sheets.

The next morning was even better. Ebony's dad made pancakes, and there was a choice of sliced banana, lemon and sugar, maple syrup, and blueberries and whipped cream. By the time Maya's dad arrived, Sasha didn't want to ever leave.

"When will your parents be coming?" Ebony's mum asked.

"Sasha said her dad's flying in from skiing in Japan," Ebony said excitedly. "And her mum's been shopping in Paris, so their chauffeur is coming to get her."

Ebony's mum's eyes widened. "Is that right?"

Sasha nodded. "But he might be late. And I know you have to go out so I'm okay to meet him in town instead."

"No, I'm sorry, but that won't be possible."

Sasha's heart quickened. "But I told him I'd meet him outside the library!"

Ebony's mum shook her head. "You're in our home and I'm responsible for you. I'm not going to let you wander off by yourself."

"Steph," Ebony's dad said in a warning tone. The adults' eyes met as if exchanging some kind of secret message. "It's okay, Sasha. You can meet the chauffeur wherever it was that you arranged."

Sasha tried to throw him a grateful look, but he wouldn't meet her eyes.

Later that afternoon, back at the camp, Magic Maggie poured Sasha a cup of peppermint tea and handed her a ginger-nut biscuit while she continued to teach her to crochet. "How was the sleepover?"

Sasha turned to Maggie and sighed. "It was like being in heaven."

Chapter 9

Liar

"Ebony!" Sasha called again, rushing to catch up. But Ebony kept walking across the schoolyard, straight to Maya. The two girls promptly turned away from Sasha.

"What's wrong?" Sasha asked.

Ebony kept her back turned as if Sasha wasn't even there, but Maya spun around. "You're a liar."

Sasha felt stunned, as if she'd been slapped.

"Mum says that you've been telling us lies," Ebony said, still not facing Sasha. "She asked a friend who's a real estate agent who knows who lives in the big houses and who doesn't."

Sasha stammered, "B-but ..."

"We know that you don't live in a mansion," Maya said. "And you don't have a French chef and your dad doesn't hang out with movie stars.

You probably live in some dumpster."

Sasha had never felt as miserable as she did that day, sitting alone in class. Mr Brock didn't have a fixed seating plan and Ebony chose to sit as far away from Sasha as she could. In the playground during break, Sasha sat by herself, barely able to eat her peanut butter sandwich.

When the bell rang for home time, Sasha didn't even bother waiting until all the other kids had left. Instead, she raced out of the gates and across town, back to the camp.

"Sa-sa!" Charlie and Lily called out with glee from the makeshift sandpit that Mum and Sasha had constructed with stones and buckets of soft sand they had scraped from the dunes.

Mum looked up and then instantly demanded, "What's wrong?"

Sasha threw down her school bag. What was wrong? Everything was wrong. Living in a car in the bushes. Not having a bed of her own. Mum being so stressed. Dad being dead. Everything was wrong! Shaking her head wordlessly, she ran to the beach.

Usually, the sparkling blue-green of the waves and fresh salty air would soothe her. But not today. Sasha huddled in the shelter and privacy of a dune, grateful for the brisk wind that allowed her to scream and sob without being heard.

Only, she had been heard.

"Sasha?"

She looked up slowly, unwilling to be distracted from the horrible howling hurt that consumed her.

Magic Maggie crouched beside her. "Want to tell me about it?"

Sasha shook her head.

"Are you sure? Sometimes talking about things can make them a whole lot less awful."

"This will never get better." Sasha choked. "I lied."

"About what?" Maggie's voice was gentle and steady. Sasha knew she would never say anything to anyone else.

"I told my friends that I lived in one of the hilltop mansions. I told them my dad was rich, that he was still …"

"Alive?"

As if a dam had burst, grief flooded through her, while Maggie sat calmly beside her, gently patting her shoulder.

Only when it had subsided and there couldn't possibly be any more tears did Maggie say, "Do you think your friends might be feeling hurt and angry because you lied to them? And that if they knew the truth, if they knew why you lied, that they might understand better?"

Sasha considered it. How would she have felt if her friends had lied to her? And if one of them had lied because she could not bear her real life, would she be mean about that, or would she try to understand?

"It's too much work to live a lie," Maggie added. "I should know that. The moment I started living as I had secretly dreamed about for all those years, everything just started to get better. These days, life feels magical."

Chapter 10

Froth

Sasha had been popular at her old school. She knew how kids punished other kids by not speaking to them. She had done it herself. Now, it took all her courage and most of the lunch break to finally approach Ebony and Maya.

Seeing their looks of disdain, Sasha blurted out desperately, "Can I talk with you please?"

Maya sniffed. "I don't think so. We don't talk to liars."

Sasha fought back tears. "I just want to say sorry. I'm sorry I lied to you, and I want to explain why."

Ebony narrowed her eyes. "Why?"

Sasha felt like she was tearing off her own skin so that the other two could see her raw and painful insides. "My dad died last year."

Ebony's eyes widened. "Why didn't you tell us?"

"I didn't want to be the girl everyone talked about and felt sorry for. If you believed that I had this great life, then maybe I could believe it, too."

"How did he die?" Maya asked, still suspicious.

Sasha took a deep breath. "No one knew it was going to happen. It was his heart. The doctor said it had been a ticking time bomb. And after that, Mum lost her job, and she couldn't afford the rent. She had a friend living here so we came up to stay with her. But that didn't work out."

Seeing Ebony and Maya's faces softening, Sasha added, "I didn't want to tell anyone. I didn't want to have to tell anyone about my dad or that we ... don't have a home."

She added quickly, "Mum's working hard to try and find somewhere for us to rent. But when I went to your house, Ebony, it was like being in heaven. Until we find a place to rent here, we're basically camping. Anyway, I know you probably don't want to be friends with me any more, but I just wanted to explain and say sorry."

The bell rang before either girl could reply, but as they filed into the classroom, Sasha was grateful to see that Ebony sat at the desk beside her.

Now that she had told the truth, it didn't matter that Mum was waiting for her at the gates after school.

"Where are the monsters?" Sasha asked.

Mum grinned. "Maggie said she'd look after them for a couple of hours. I thought we should spend some time together. Just you and me."

Sasha stiffened. Had Maggie told Mum about what had happened? About the kind of lies she'd told to Ebony and Maya? But Mum wasn't saying anything. Instead, she stopped at a cafe. "Why don't we get something to drink? What would you like?"

Sasha knew this was an extravagance. Mum needed to be saving every single cent she could for the rental bond and deposit. "Don't we need to be saving?"

Mum shrugged. "I've got together enough for the bond, and today I made three rental applications! I don't know what our chances are, but I'm crossing fingers. I think we should celebrate." She added, "Hot chocolate with marshmallows?"

Sasha's mouth fell open.

Mum laughed. "Sasha Bear, you think I didn't know about your secret Sunday sugar hits?

Dad and I always told each other everything."

They sat outside, basking in the sunshine. Light bounced off the river as it flowed past at high tide, while Sasha used a teaspoon to scrape up the last of the froth.

"I want to thank you," Mum said. "You've been such a great help to me. It hasn't been easy, and I haven't always been able to be there for you like I would have wished." She blinked fiercely, holding back tears. "You know, all I ever wanted for my daughter, my children, was for them to have what I didn't: a loving, stable home. Two parents and a safe place to all be together and make memories. Never in my wildest dreams did I think that this could happen."

Sasha licked the last bit of melted marshmallow off her spoon. "I really wish Dad was still here. But it's going to be okay," she said.

As Mum reached across the table and squeezed her hand, Sasha was surprised to find she wasn't just lying to make her mother feel better.

Somehow, at this moment in time, suspended between the warm afternoon light and the shimmer of the river, she felt the worry and sadness ebbing away. They were moving on.

"We're still making memories, Mum," Sasha said. "Just different ones."